D0783208

## BY DAVID WAGONER

*Poems*
Dry Sun, Dry Wind (1953)
A Place to Stand (1958)
The Nesting Ground (1963)
Staying Alive (1966)
New and Selected Poems (1969)
Riverbed (1972)
Sleeping in the Woods (1974)
Travelling Light (1976)
Collected Poems 1956–1976 (1976)
Who Shall Be the Sun? (1978)
In Broken Country (1979)
Landfall (1981)

*Novels*
The Man in the Middle (1954)
Money Money Money (1955)
Rock (1958)
The Escape Artist (1965)
Baby, Come on Inside (1968)
Where Is My Wandering Boy Tonight? (1970)
The Road to Many a Wonder (1974)
Tracker (1975)
Whole Hog (1976)
The Hanging Garden (1980)

*Edited*
Straw for the Fire: From the Notebooks of Theodore Roethke,
    1943–1963 (1972)

# *Landfall*

◎⋉⋈⋉⋈⋉⋈◎

# *Landfall*

*POEMS*

David Wagoner

◎⋉⋈⋉⋈⋉⋈◎

*An Atlantic Monthly Press Book*
Little, Brown and Company        Boston        Toronto

FIRST EDITION

For Acknowledgments see page 111

*Library of Congress Cataloging in Publication Data*

Wagoner, David.
  Landfall: poems.

  "An Atlantic Monthly Press book."
  I. Title.
PS3545.A345L3   811'.54   80-25313
ISBN 0-316-91706-0
ISBN 0-316-91707-9 (pbk.)

ATLANTIC—LITTLE, BROWN BOOKS
ARE PUBLISHED BY
LITTLE, BROWN AND COMPANY
IN ASSOCIATION WITH
THE ATLANTIC MONTHLY PRESS

MV

*Designed by Janis Capone*

*Published simultaneously in Canada
by Little, Brown & Company (Canada) Limited*

PRINTED IN THE UNITED STATES OF AMERICA

For Patt,
downstream and upstream,
with love

ဢဢ

# CONTENTS

## One

## Two

*Three*

# One

## ‮ﬗ‬

### *Under the Sign of Moth*

Having read and written myself almost to sleep, I stretch
Toward the light and see it
There on the otherwise bare ceiling:
A rust-and-black-winged moth
Motionless over our heads, waiting for something —
The scent of a distant, screened-off mate? Some hint
Of a flower to feed on? Another chrysalis?

My wife is already sleeping, not knowing
We will spread our dreams under the Sign of Moth,
A constellation presiding over us
(More plausibly than the thread-spinning of stars
That housed our births) by clinging
Somehow to the plaster heaven we trusted
To see us safely and vacantly through the night.

I turn out the lamp that might have tempted it
To flutter down and play its familiar role
As a fool for brightness, a hopeful dabbler
Aspiring long enough to expire, battered
And singed by what it thought it wanted,
To suffer a last demeaning transformation
Into a moral lesson.

In the near-darkness, its eyes catch at the streetlight
And gleam deep red, lidlessly staring
Downward at the beginning of our sleep.
What can I offer it but peace and quiet?
With heavy eyelids, I return its gaze

More and more heavily, now blinking, my body
Unable to rise to this occasion,

Either to hunt for love or food or light
Or to fashion a moth-net from some gauzy remnant
Or to manage anything but a spinning fall
Into a dream of becoming
A shape that wants to leave old forms behind,
Now hidden, now crawling upward, now flying,
Endlessly new, endlessly unfolding.

The ceiling is blank in the morning.
I yawn and slip out from under, obeying the obscure
Scheme of the day, drifting from room to room.
The moth is somewhere in a dusty crevice,
Its long tongue coiled more certainly than a spring
Made to keep time, still waiting
For what it came to find and will die for.

## Falling Asleep in a Garden

All day the bees have come to the garden.
They hover, swivel in arcs and, whirling, light
On stamens heavy with pollen, probe and revel
Inside the yellow and red starbursts of dahlias
Or cling to lobelia's blue-white mouths
Or climb the speckled trumpets of foxgloves.

My restless eyes follow their restlessness
As they plunge bodily headfirst into treasure,
Gold-fevered among these horns of plenty.
They circle me, a flowerless patch
With nothing to offer them in the way of sweetness
Or light against the first omens of evening.

Some, even now, are dying at the end
Of their few weeks, some being born in the dark,
Some simply waiting for life, but some are dancing
Deep in their hives, telling the hungry
*The sun will be that way, the garden this far:*
*This is the way to the garden.* They hum at my ear.

And I wake up, startled, seeing the early
Stars beginning to bud in constellations.
The bees have gathered somewhere like petals closing
For the coming of the cold. The silhouette
Of a sphinx moth swerves to drink at a flowerhead.
The night-blooming moon opens its pale corolla.

ൠ

*Caterpillar Song*

Summer and leaves filled me
With a green drowse, now full
Of sleep I must turn
Leaflike, the fine thread
Comes from my lower lip
And fastens to a leaf, I am
Weaving around my fullness
A closing, a slow shuttling
To touch there and there
Where I will dream
All my hearts withering
And changing to a half-remembered
One in the air who quivers
Among leaves, who will know
Night after night by this
Night I spin around us how
Already it stirs
From sleep inside me, gathers
The leaves I have left
In me, how we begin
Together, it grows huge eyes
For me, and we wait
Behind them, it is growing
Shut wings, we wait between them
Night by night after this
Night spun around us, we know
Now is the time to soften
The way ahead for us, it opens,
The wet shut wings come slowly
Out, they open, the veins

Fill them, they harden
And belong to us, we see
The night with all our eyes
At once, we move our wings
Apart among leaves, the one
Leaf with eyes to open
The night, not falling now
But rising and flying.

ဢ

*Spider Song*

It flies crookedly
For its food toward the heart
Of color. It will be bound
To touch my colorless
Round thin web-flower
Where I wait at the center
At ease even with wind.
And it comes now, caught
By the fine-spun petals
Where it waits, where it beats
Its wings. It waits
While I dance to help it
Wait, to learn to become
Something far different.
I hold it at the ends
Of what I am. It learns
To turn in one direction
Only, only to spin
One way under my eyes.
It learns to love
What is pale and quiet,
Near, motionless,
Whatever is here. It forgets
All those further places
That made it thrash and flutter.
It learns those wings
Were meant to bring it here.
It learns stillness. It turns
For a last time into me.

ᘏᘉ

## Moth Song

I tasted it, the gold
In the gold, I saw the sweetness
At the end of my uncoiling
Tongue, by the beautiful ends
Of what curved from my forehead,
And I swam, gliding, I dove
Through the air toward gold
And sweetness meant to be
Chosen, begging to hold me
And be drawn inside me.

But I stop now, I hang
Still, suddenly suspended
Without having chosen to be
Still in a breeze still full
Of calling and beckoning
Red and blue around gold,
And what comes to meet me
Holds me and turns
My body, spinning a lightness
Around me to fold my wings
Close into a darkness,
And it turns me slowly
Into a flower and drinks me,
And I open, I become
Completely known, I blossom.

## My Fire

In the cave under our house
I tended the fire: a furnace
Where black fossils of ferns
And swamp-shaking dinosaurs
Would burn through the cold mornings
If I shook the dying and dead
Ashes down through the grate
And, with firetongs, hauled out clinkers
Like the vertebrae of monsters.

I made my magic there,
Not the bloody charms of hunters,
Not shamans or animals
Painted on damp walls,
But something from fire. My father
Tended huge rows of fires
And burned with them all day,
Sometimes all evening, all night
In a steelmill, brought fire home
On his face and his burnt skin
And slept, glowing dark red.

My fire made steam in coils
And pipes and radiators
Poured from the steel he made
Somewhere I'd only seen
Far off, the burning mountains
Where God kept His true flame
To Himself, melting and turning

Blood-colored ore to pigs
And men to something stranger.

My spirit would swell and sing
Inside those pipes, would knock
And rattle to be let out,
Would circle through walls and floors,
Turn back to water and fall
To the fire again, turn white,
Rise hissing in every room
Against the windows to grow
Fronds and bone-white flowers,
All ice in a frozen garden.

ᎳᏫ

## My Path

Each morning, going to school,
I walked through ragweed, sandburs,
Odd weed-crowns, all ragtail
Outcasts like the bums
In the beckoning, forbidden
Hooverville by the railroad,
And going home each evening
Across that lot (between mounds
Where someone started a house
But left it to go wild)
I lingered, feeling vacant
Between lessons on thrift,
On keeping clean and keeping
Quiet, on speaking up,
On speaking when spoken to,
On keeping time. The weeds
Kept their own time: some fell
In snow and rose in the rain,
Some hitched long rides, some cracked
Open and flew sideways,
Some twisted and writhed on end
Till they turned under ground,
Some could drift on the wind,
And all took beatings easy:
They moved back for a while,
Then moved in or moved on.
I made a path among them,
Learning their hard homework.

ကၺ

*Weeds*

Crabgrass, ragweed, sandbur, plantain — I knew them
Better than lawnkeepers knew their favorite
Square green grassbeds, better than gentlemen
Of the turf knew edgers or rollers, clippers or sprinklers
Whose neat bushes of water played
More usefully than we did.

In vacant lots and the cracks of concrete, we flourished
As unobtrusively as we could, and as fast,
In holes no one remembered digging, from decaying
Compost heaps nobody ever used
To feed the gardens weeds had been born in,
From which they were exiled.

We never seemed out of place to me. I grew
Invisibly like them by alleys, in gutters,
At the ends of streets that no one superintended,
By railroad beds — a tumbleweed ready to break
Away forever between dry roots
And stem-base, joining the wind.

ꔍ

## My Father's Garden

On his way to the open hearth where white-hot steel
Boiled against furnace walls in wait for his lance
To pierce the fire-clay and set loose demons
And dragons in molten tons, blazing
Down to the huge satanic cauldrons,
Each day he would pass the scrapyard, his kind of garden.

In rusty rockeries of stoves and brake-drums,
In grottoes of sewing machines and refrigerators,
He would pick flowers for us: small gears and cogwheels
With teeth like petals, with holes for anthers,
Long stalks of lead to be poured into toy soldiers,
Ball-bearings as big as grapes to knock them down.

He was called a melter. He tried to keep his brain
From melting in those tyger-mouthed mills
Where the same steel reappeared over and over
To be reborn in the fire as something better
Or worse: cannons or cars, needles or girders,
Flagpoles, swords, or ploughshares.

But it melted. His classical learning ran
Down and away from him, not burning bright.
His fingers culled a few cold scraps of Latin
And Greek, *magna sine laude,* for crosswords
And brought home lumps of tin and sewer grills
As if they were his ripe prize vegetables.

ૹ

## My Father's Ghost

If you count nine stars and nine stones, then look into an empty
room, you'll see a ghost.

— MIDWESTERN FOLK BELIEF

I counted them, and now I look through the door
Into the empty room where he was, where nine stars
Have failed to conjure him under a ceiling
Presiding over nothing except a floor
And four walls without windows, where nine stones
Have failed to call him up from the netherworld
To tell me of his cruel unnatural murder.

He stays as invisible as other souls
In either world. I have to imagine him
In this interior without natural light,
Recall him burned by splashing steel each shift
Of his unnatural life, his thigh broken
To an Oedipal limp, his eyes half-blinded
By staring into the pits of open hearths,
His memory put to sleep, his ears deafened
By the slamming of drop-forges and the roar
Of fire as bright as the terrible hearts of stars,
Of fire that would melt stones. He won't come back
At anyone's bidding in his hard-hat of a helmet,
His goggles up like a visor, but I dream him
Returning unarmed, unharmed. Words, words. I hold
My father's ghost in my arms in his dark doorway.

15

ಬಿ

*Elegy Written in a Suburban Churchyard*

No curfew and no room for the complaints
Of owls this evening, not even bats: no belfry.
And no one plodding on foot, only the herds
Of cars geared up for home, thanking God it's Friday.

They haven't left me the world, but they leave me
Sitting inside this Presbyterian graveyard,
One of the few not spirited out of town
As the dead give up the right-of-way to nightfall.

St. John, St. Paul, St. George — the Beatles are droning
In the basement where the young are living it up,
Slamming their discos down on empty squares,
Ringo instead of bingo drumming the numbers.

To judge by the punched memorial beercans,
They know these markers better than I do
And treat their texts like sermons on readerboards.
They take them and leave them. Names and dates are boring.

The only inevitable hour they've known so far
Is the next one. Paths of glory? For psychopaths.
Their world's still short on Hampdens and Cromwells.
They can't tell Milton from a hole in the ground.

These holes in the ground are covered with dry cheatgrass
And nettles and genuine blooming pink wild roses.
Here, bromegrass, taking the measure of Simon Corl,
Has choked itself in his memory like his memory.

The spike-topped wrought-iron pickets standing threefold
By Jenny Calder Banyard are rusting away
Gracefully, turning graceful hydrangeas blue
(As her eyes once must have been) with iron oxide.

Is it so hard to lie down? Sometimes it's hard
Naming the difference between life and death
And harder to tell the living from the dying.
Most people shuffle along at some of both.

So far, no one has caught me. Did Thomas Gray
Worry whether the peasants would think him tetched,
Foolish, or ghoulish, mooning in cemeteries?
No sergeants or sextons, switching their blue blinkers

Or flashlights into my eyes have come to grill me.
But if they do, I'm ready with an answer:
My blind Great-uncle Simon wrote a book
In his old age called *The Wildflowers of Ohio*,

And Grandmother Jenny sang on the day she died.
Not far from the madding crowd, I came on purpose
To find their epitaphs, and write one, but couldn't
Make any worth their time except *Good Night*.

ᄭᄭ

*In the Country of Old Men*

He woke in a different country, his own hands
Rose to his mouth, and his fingers
Rubbed at his eyes, and he was standing
On his own feet, but the people passing
Had darkened their speech like daylight going dim
Around him, he told them to speak slowly, he told them
To listen, please, he told them he was trying
To understand and be patient, if only
They would be more understandable, something was coming
Between them, something as ordinary
As a shadow, he didn't know why, but it was growing
Darker too suddenly, they were walking and talking
Too quickly, too softly, and he didn't want them
Thinking the worst of him, but would they mind
Saying just once more whatever it was
They were saying, and he would do his best to think
Of an answer, but their eyes were turning
Away wide open in some other direction
For some other purpose, they were going on purpose
Somewhere else he didn't happen to be
Going, not having any reason to go there,
So he took his time and watched them blur and fade,
And he kept quiet and decided to wait, to lie
Down and be still and listen, to learn how.

ʓʓ

*For a Root-bound Rosebush*

They grew where they could, the roots
Of this yellow rose, recircling
The shut circumference of a world
Made out of clay, all interweaving
Till they could find and hold
Only themselves, and again themselves.

And again I move their intricate mass
Into a slightly larger darkness
Where they will search once more
For the ends of their earth
While the buds above them in the sun
Open and close the eyes of summer.

ରୁବ୍ର

*Cutworm*

I found him clinging to roots in a flowerbed,
Pale body gleaming and curled at the beginning
Of his day of dreaming under the stalks and leaves
He had spent the whole night mouthing and mulling over.

He lay there full of flowers I had hoped to cut
Myself, the buds of white petunias surging
In his fat body, arranging his life in secret
For the start of spring, for his first flight as a moth.

And without thinking, I threw him out of the garden,
Tossed him over the fence and, after him,
The flower he'd lived by, and watched them flying,
Falling through berry vines, where I can't reach them.

My impulse was to grudge him his small share
Of a world I've wished for. Now I wish him well
After the fact. May he and the flower together
Grow in that wilderness of thorns and fruit.

May he become his flying self or be eaten
By a wren or a raven (though those great expectations
Must have seemed cold comfort once to Christians
As they waited too short a time for the lions).

May he become, if he can, the Moth of Moths,
A swift pale-brown tailspinning dodger of bats,
The Grand Godfather Cutworm in whose mouth
The Petunia of Petunias will be translated.

## Squirrel

He carries his horse-chestnut like a thief
With a sack of gold in a fairy tale,
Looking for somewhere safe enough
To bury the good life.

He stops to stare, wondering whether
I can be trusted to know his hiding place
Or whether, like Ali Baba eavesdropping,
I'll learn his secret and rob him later.

Thinking of winter too, I outwait
The attention he pays to us
Unreliable paymasters and keepers,
Past-masters of the empty handout.

He gives me, at long last, the benefit
Of his doubt: in the loam
By a rosebush, digging as knowingly
As a gardener, he either stores

(In case he lives to remember)
Or plants (if he forgets or dies)
A small feast — or a tree that will bear proof
Against winter longer than almost any story.

## For a Jumping Spider

This jumping spider and I are taking the sun
Together: he, reckless as a high-steel worker
In scorn of all hard-hatted safety rules,
Ruling the slippery roost of my deck chair,
And I, flat out in gravity's safekeeping,
      Held up in the air by scaffolding.

On six of his eight legs (with two foot-feelers
Leading the way), calmly he reconnoiters
Sideways or upside down the rack and webbing
We share for all our devious purposes:
Hunger for food, hunger for light, and hunger
      For one more memorable evening.

He has crawled close to my shoulder. I admire
The iridescent opacity of his eyes,
All eight, including the smallest pair
In the back of his broad, eighth-of-an-inch head,
His beard bristling as purply as his body
      Around a mouth mock-solemnly down-turning.

He preens those whiskers with his pedipalps
And crouches an inch from my strange territory:
That sunny slope down which saltwater, streaming
To no good purpose, must look as uninviting
As a desert shimmering and blurred by mirages
      Where nothing is worth having or hunting.

But with a touch of his spinnerets, he anchors
His lifeline and jumps toward skin, breaking the world's

Comparative standing-broadjump record (Wingless
Division), all the way to my elbow, which in-
Voluntarily jerks and sends him careening
        On purpose, with his own dead-aiming,

Upside-slantwise onto my icy glass
Where he clings, reconsiders, anchors again, then jumps
Back to the sloping backrest, utterly
Casual as he cuts the line, now zigzagged
Behind him, a tracery with the impermanence
        And after-sheen of lightning.

I go on basking as purposefully as I can,
Blinking, remembering night, trying to remember
Anything easy to forget, hunting for something
New under sun or moon to fill me, and he
With his unblinkable eyes scuttles toward shade,
        Staring, forgetting nothing, searching.

ಬೆ

*Nuthatch*

Quick, at the feeder, pausing
Upside down, in its beak
A sunflower seed held tight
To glance by chestnut, dust-blue,
White, an eye-streak
Gone in a blurred ripple
Straight to the cedar branch
To the trunk to a crevice
In bark and putting it
In there, quick, with the others,
Then arrowing straight back
For just one more all morning.

## The Young Clematis (Clematis verticillaris)

An inch a day, it climbs the fan-shaped trellis,
Each pair of leaves with stems like tendrils
Clutching at latticework, lifting through light
And spiralling, shadowed, taking whole afternoons
To decide what to depend on, lingering
Over each careful, thread-thin, seasoned gesture,
Then slowly spreading wide, no longer Climber
But Keeper whose hard tasks are clinging for life
All fall, all winter, all spring, harder than weather,
Then bursting with blue flowers through the dead of summer.

## ∞

*Wild Clematis* (Clematis paniculata)


Without clinging or winding, it sends long shoots
Up through the branches of a tree, branching
Itself behind sunlight, secretly interweaving
Among stiff twigs and stems and mounting
The scaffold it depends on and will hang from,
Searching along the limbs of its skeleton
And lifting itself to the light at the treecrown
Where it spreads out suddenly like a garland
Burgeoning, bursting wide, casting downwind
Its feathery white seeds and killing what holds it,
What rots away under it and topples. From the wreckage
Of vines, the shoots come groping, dreaming of climbing.

ເຄ

## The Garden of Earthly Delights
after the painting by Hieronymus Bosch

We stand in bright pools together, waiting with crows,
Some with white egrets, and some with leaf-winged apples.
Among us, our dark sisters. Some few are drowning,
But what does it matter? We are beautiful,
Our smooth temptations, our whiteness and blackness
Are being praised by the Pride of the Peacock,
And around us an endless penitent festival
Is riding its bears and camels, lions and goats,
Wild boars, gryphons, and unicorns, with roses deeper
Than our dreams, huge fish as emblems,
And the unbreakable egg of the Bird of Love.

Beyond them, the rarest birds, alertly at peace,
Larger than mere life, attend our pageant.
They see us born out of mussels and weedcrowns,
They see a few returning to sleep in shells,
They share the enormous berries we have learned
To crave as they do, to cling to, to carry
From one place to another, the dangling grapes
Which taught us to cluster, ripen, and drink
(Like moths from wild thistles) only to ourselves.

Why should we care what birds may want from us?
They have it at will, the seeds, the softening flesh
Of apples, strawberry beds, the arbors
Whose grapes burn dark as the moon on the other
Side of this earth that has made us the chosen
Attendants of its ceremonial daylight.
We live and die here hourly. We burn, we drift
From one invisible fire to the next, we fondle

What feeds our loving mouths with the first silence
We gave to what first gave us sweetness and sadness.

And we dance among them and find each other's bodies
Standing or lying down, all growing like fruit
And moving, swelling in this perpetual season
Of our fulfillment into comfortable Death
Whose towers we delight to climb, the pink and blue
Marble and flowering turrets risen from water
Like five Fortunate Islands where no laughter
Spills or gathers or takes leave of our senses.

Some idly take to the air as birds and go
Wherever they wish, some perch to wait our pleasure
Or take the paths all creatures, like constellations,
Take at their peril in this day with no evening,
This constant day in sheltered estuaries
We could visit easily if we wished to begin
Walking among the safely grazing and browsing
Beasts of the field and orchard and far forest.

Instead, we will stay here and become nothing
But what we are, the careless gardeners
Who scarcely touch the earth, who never smile.
Even the drowned, the confined, the suspended
Hold their unsmiling faces still forever.

*Two*

ನಃ

## Song from the Second Floor

"If you can't think, at least sing."
— ROETHKE

And I can't think for all the wind and rain
Pummelling the windows,
For the sight of the salmon-trunked, deep-olive-leaved
Madroña beside the house
Pitching half over, rearing upright again,
Storm-dancing all morning
As, piecemeal, the ruck of fall is blowing away,
Flung past but lingering,
All of it tumbling and falling, rising, spinning through mist,
The stems and feathers,
Hailstones like winged seeds, the seeds in showers,
The latter-day tatters
Of leaves and needles, the husks of ash and hazel
Light-spun, rushing northeast
Together at last and again, becoming each other
Again and at wild last
In all this melting air and flying water
Sailing and singing.

ᘚ

*Whisper Song*


Listening and listening
Closely, you may hear
(After its other
Incredibly clear song)
The one the winter wren
Sings in the thinnest of whispers
More quietly than soft rain
Proclaiming almost nothing
To itself and to you,
And you must be
Only a step away
To hear it even faintly
(No one knows why
It will sing so softly),
Its tiny claws
Braced for arpeggios,
Its dark eyes
Gleaming with a small
Astonishing promise,
Its beak held open
For its hushed throat,
Whispering to itself
From its mysterious heart.

## Cuckoo

"The man that invented the cuckoo clock is dead. It is old news, but there is nothing else the matter with it."

— MARK TWAIN

Both doors of this clock stand frozen open: in one, a cuckoo
Stuck on a missing note; in the other, two hand-carved peasants,
Their dance suspended in mid-whirl. The hunter's horn,
The rifles, the strung-up hare and grouse, the stag's head
Have been joined by the music box in their dead silence.
The whole *Tickenmitklingelnkuckuck* stopped cold at midnight.

For years it played its Bavarian schmaltz on the hour and half hour
When the cuckoo had had its say, while Dirndl and Leather Britches
Spun in a dutiful pretense of *Gemütlichkeit*.
We had to hoist the pinecone weights, drag three chains down
Twice daily to keep their acts up to the mark. *Gott sei dank,*
Something has finally gone kaput with this clockmaker's nightmare.

In the Black Forest of *our* nightmares, we could half hear it
Celebrating its openhanded notions of time: thirteen
For three, an extra helping for four, and sometimes
Nothing but music for any odd hour, maybe the bird
Sleeping it off behind that slaphappy doorway
Full of slipped cogs and wooden teeth, a flophouse for gnomes.

It's as unforgettable as a trauma and has to be doctored
By some jolly, jowly offspring of the Brothers Grimm.
Meanwhile, we'll lie down without it and be cuckoo all night,
Bird-brained as ever, listening, stiffer than trophies,
Two substitute dancers twirling through the dark, rolled over
And over the barrel, miscounting slugabed heartbeats.

33

ಬಿಡಿ

*Quiet*

"The amount of quiet I need is not to be found on the face of the earth."
— KAFKA

His was a barking-dog's world, a cellblock of plaster-
And-lath retreats where windows and doors, even locked,
Shook with the outcries of machines, where strangers
Mumbled breakable oaths, and a goulash of music
Poured through downspouts and drains into his ears.

He stopped those ears with wax, but the hum of his nerves
Made every room a hive where, dancing all night
Across the ceiling, prisoners in the attic
Rehearsed the rediscovery of lost gardens.
How could he hear himself think when he could hear

Even his own breathing, heart beating, the scratching
Of pen across paper like a fingernail?
Then came the bells in the high thick houses of God
And Mammon proclaiming, claiming another hour
With clappers chained head-down in their bronze dungeons.

꙾

*The Arsonist*

He steps down into the darkness, dreaming
Already of the seeds he will plant there,
The red and yellow shoots
That will grow more wildly than flowers in a real garden,
That will bloom for him alone,

That will turn at the touch of fingers, budding and climbing
Through all four seasons, deepening
Their blackened roots
As they lift their more and more perfectly dazzling
Flowerheads, his alone.

They are mounting the bare walls now, the living vines
Clinging, devouring, interlaced like veins
Binding his bare bones
With blood-red tendrils. The windows of his eyes
Catch fire. Trembling alone,

He watches bright petals bursting against the sky.
He smiles for the mourners wailing, coming to see
At a hearth his other body
Bringing its light to the world, uprisen and dying
For love, no longer alone.

ෆෆ

*The Shooting Lesson*

No one can hold a firearm absolutely
Still: our arms waver,
No matter how steady, steady we seem standing
In a field with nothing
To brace us like stones or trees, but we may bear
Down on natural trembling
By sitting or lying prone, no shakier now
Than the earth, which stays as is
Long enough to support us while we hold
Our breath, doing our best
To squeeze this shot without thinking about it,
Not yanking the trigger
Merely because we feel we need more air.
Our weapon must appear
To go off by itself in what we call
*Surprise fire.*
Whether our target is running or holding still,
Our aim should be the aim
Of a lifetime, all our habits rolled into one
Object on one straight line
With eyes not squinting or narrowed but held wide open
Over our open sights
So that nothing could be more open-mouthed than we are
To see the final results.

ᔕᔕ

*Palindrome: Inside Out*

Cat loves mouse
(If death is romance)
And pat and pounce
Become kiss and caress,
But caress and kiss
Become pounce and pat,
And romance is death
If mouse loves cat.

ಋ

*My Physics Teacher*

He tried to convince us, but his billiard ball
Fell faster than his pingpong ball and thumped
To the floor first, in spite of Galileo.
The rainbows from his prism skidded off-screen
Before we could tell an infra from an ultra.
His hand-cranked generator refused to spit
Sparks and settled for smoke. The dangling pith
Ignored the attractions of his amber wand,
No matter how much static he rubbed and dubbed
From the seat of his pants, and the housebrick
He lowered into a tub of water weighed
(Eureka!) more than the overflow.

He believed in a World of Laws, where problems had answers,
Where tangible objects and intangible forces
Acting thereon could be lettered, numbered, and crammed
Through our tough skulls for lifetimes of homework.
But his only uncontestable demonstration
Came with our last class: he broke his chalk
On a formula, stooped to catch it, knocked his forehead
On the eraser-gutter, staggered slewfoot, and stuck
One foot forever into the wastebasket.

১৩

*In Distress*

(Selected entirely from *International Code of Signals,* United States Edition, published by U.S. Naval Oceanographic Office)

I am abandoning my vessel
Which has suffered a nuclear accident
And is a possible source of radiation danger.
    *You should abandon your vessel as quickly as possible.*
    *Your vessel will have to be abandoned.*
I shall abandon my vessel
Unless you will remain by me,
Ready to assist.
I have had a serious nuclear accident
And you should approach with caution.
The position of the accident is marked by flame.
The position of the accident is marked by wreckage.
I need a doctor. I have severe burns.
I need a doctor. I have radiation casualties.
I require a helicopter urgently, with a doctor.
The number of injured or dead is not yet known.
Your aircraft should endeavor to alight
Where a flag is waved or a light is shown.
Shall I train my searchlight nearly vertical
On a cloud intermittently and, if I see your aircraft,
Deflect the beam upwind and on the water
To facilitate your landing?
    *I do not see any light.*
You may alight on my deck; I am ready to receive you forward.
You may alight on my deck; I am ready to receive you amidship.
You may alight on my deck; I am ready to receive you aft.

*I am entering a zone of restricted visibility.*
*Visibility is decreasing.*
*You should come within visual signal distance.*
I require immediate assistance; I have a dangerous list.
I require immediate assistance; I have damaged steering gear.
I require immediate assistance; I have a serious disturbance on board.
I require immediate assistance; I am on fire.
*What assistance do you require?*
*Can you proceed without assistance?*
*Boats cannot be used because of weather conditions.*
*Boats cannot be used on the starboard side because of list.*
*Boats cannot be used on the port side because of list.*
*Boats cannot be used to disembark people.*
*Boats cannot be used to get alongside.*
*Boats cannot be used to reach you.*
*I cannot send a boat.*
I require immediate assistance; I am drifting.
I am breaking adrift. I have broken adrift.
I am sinking.
*Did you see the vessel sink?*
*Is it confirmed that the vessel has sunk?*
*What is the depth of water where the vessel sank?*
*Where did the vessel sink?*
*I have lost sight of you.*
My position is doubtful.
My position is ascertained by dead reckoning.
Will you give me my position?
*You should indicate your position by searchlight.*
*You should indicate your position by smoke signal.*
*You should indicate your position by rockets or flares.*
My position is marked by flame.
My position is marked by wreckage.
Are you in the search area?
*I am in the search area.*
Are you continuing to search?
*Do you want me to continue to search?*
*I cannot continue to search.*

I cannot save my vessel.
Keep as close as possible.
I wish some persons taken off.
A skeleton crew will remain on board.
You should give immediate assistance to pick up survivors.
You should try to obtain from survivors all possible information.
*I cannot take off persons.*
*There are indications of an intense depression forming.*
*The wind is expected to veer.*
*You should take appropriate precautions.*
*A phenomenal wave is expected.*
*I cannot proceed to the rescue.*
*I will keep close to you during the night.*
*Nothing can be done until daylight.*

## Time Off for Good Behavior

*Adult:* What happens to your heart when you go to sleep?
*Child:* It stops.

— From an Interview on a
Seattle Radio Station

Of course it stops. If you lie down
In the dark, your heart unburdens itself
As gladly as you, taking small comfort
From what you manage to dream, not beating
(Since you're no longer there to listen)
At the cage-bars of your breastbone.

Why should it throb all night without you?
All day, telling itself its time
Is passing, passing away, it counted
On you to be different, not the grudging
And bloody-minded, skin-tight jailor
Making his rounds, jangling his key-ring.

But you did nothing new to persuade it
Hearts must earn their keep in the night
To be pardoned someday, forgiven, even
Given away for good to someone.
So it waits for that moment when you fall
Asleep, off-guard. Then it stops cold.

ℜℜ

## *Applying for a Loan with the Help of the* Dictionary of Occupational Titles

"You're a *what?*"
— QUESTION FROM A CREDIT MANAGER

In my other lives, I've been a sheepskin pickler,
A bowling-ball engraver, a feather washer,
Banana dispatcher, and wild cherry dipper.
I've been a bologna lacer and beeswax bleacher.
I've balanced fans, dried germs, and dipped balloons,
Served as a bellyman and a skull grinder
And saved my bacon once as a butt presser.

I've tackled even more mysterious Labors:
I've been a burning foreman, an apron scratcher,
Bar creaser, chill man, backside polisher,
Flyaway clerk, head chiseler, lingo cleaner,
Crotch joiner, hardness tester, and beat-out boy,
So don't go thinking, because I say I'm a poet,
Sir, I don't know serious work pays off.

## ∽

*Two Epitaphs*

*For a Ballet Dancer*

Her body was her instrument. Strictly on beat,
She called its tune and its turn from head to toe.
Death's unfair play is playing turnabout
Offbeat, off point, offstage: one strict tableau.

*For a Birdwatcher*

He does what he loved to do: holds still, stares up
And makes no noise, breathlessly holds his breath
And stays invisible, a part of the landscape
Among the singers over and under earth.

ᎶᎧ

## The Last Laugh

1

"Never miss a chance to laugh aloud. Smiling is better than nothing, and
a chuckle is better still — but *out and out* laughter is the real thing. Try
it now if you dare! And when you've done it, analyze your feelings."
— Douglas Fairbanks, Sr., *Laugh and Live*

I tried it just now, and our dog is staring
At my red face, alert for trouble, ready
To run for cover under the porch, and a pigeon
Just came bailing out of the holly tree
As if it had heard gunfire, and my wife is peeking
Out of an upstairs window at me, worried,
And my neighbor has flipped the switch of his Weed Eater
And is looking around, afraid something has flipped
In it or his head. I smile at one and all
Lamely (it's better than nothing) and whistle lightly
And take a mock-swashbuckling stroll among roses.

Dear Doug, wild swinger from balconies, now grinning
From your grave, no doubt (that's better than nothing too),
Maybe it helped your career and your digestion
As you say, but if laughing's the Wine of Life
And of Love Life, et cetera, where do I go from here?
The dog, the pigeon, my wife, and my neighbor
Are only now getting back to what passes
For normal these days, and they and I are still
Stuck with your idea, hearing that dreadful
Gurgling sour-mashed sole-squashed grapeskinny laughter

That poured out of my belly, too weak for a wineskin,
That spilled from my throat as if from a bad year
When something awful watered the grapevines.


2


".  .  . get out into the open air. Run down the street and if possible
out into the country. If we see a tree and have the inclination to climb
it — well, then climb it."

— IBID.

I got here the easy way (I admit it), in high gear,
Not running, and I'm looking at more trees
Than anyone but a logger knows what to do with,
And I stand at the foot of one: trunk not too big
Around for a bear-hug, first branch not out of reach,
And bark no worse than a love-bite for my palms.

I remember climbing trees in my beardless youth,
Not simply to get away from watchdogs or farmers
Or bulls or bullies, but to get away
From it all, thinking of Errol Flynn and Tarzan
Or your own son, Doug, who did his share of climbing
And running around and swinging, always good

For a laugh. I have a peculiar inclination
To lean against this tree, to sit beside it,
To make my peace with it, to try thinking
What I'm doing out here in the country, to try
Figuring out what all these trees are doing
Which, to judge by the stumps, is no laughing matter.

". . . if it is night when you run across these lines, drop this book and trot yourself around the block a few times. Then come back and you'll enjoy it more than otherwise."

— IBID.

Doug, it left me as breathless
As your prose and your two ideas:
Do It and Then Do It
Again, No Matter What May Come
To Mind While You're Doing It.
Believe me, neither your book
Nor I seem any better
Than before I ran around
My block, not laughing
Once to put some jogger,
Mugger, or timid burglar
Off his midnight stride,
And now I stretch out flat
In the darkness to recover
In love and sleep and fear
And anger, some better humor.

**ဢ**

*Bears*


Out of shadows as deep as shadows
In the woods, the bears come swaying
On their hindlegs, the black pads
Of forepaws reaching forward, their foreheads
Higher than all the men now running
Behind them into the charmed circle,
Into the ring and the glaring spotlight,
Now pausing, lifting their muzzles, turning
To a blare of horns, they begin dancing
At the ends of leashes, their fur gleaming
All shades of fallen leaves by moonlight,
Up on red globes and walking, not falling
Off, they waddle steadily, swiftly
To the feet of silver trees and climb them
To other trees, descending, they swivel
Firesticks in their claws, they ride
On wheels so surely, so heavily
They seem to spiral downward without
Stopping, and now they are swaying away
On sawdust to drumbeats, to applause
Like heartbeats while men are running behind them
Becoming shadows again among shadows.

∞

*Games*

The children from the nursery school are running
Slowly, zigzaggedly on the grass at the zoo,
Trying to catch the chickens that run free
Among the bushes and always get away.

The game is called Chasing Something. You play it
Squawking and clucking, wonderfully unhappy
Not to be able to touch those feathers ruffling
And flapping, squawking back at you out of fear.

You wear your name and the name of your keeper
And don't pay any attention to each other
Or to lions or llamas or boas or kangaroos.
You want your game to be right out in the open

Where you can reach for it with friendly fingers
And crow out loud to say how eager you are,
How hungry to learn a game called Catching Something.
But if you catch it, then what do you do?

Do you start a zoo and fill it with wild playthings
Waiting behind bars to look at children
Chasing more chickens under the mapletrees?
You don't catch anything yet. Keepers catch *you.*

They make you sit together and play Yelling
And Eating and Drinking and Dropping Sandwiches.
The chickens gather around you quietly
And play their game called Come to the Picnic.

ૹૹ

*Peacock*

Over the clipped lawn, grandly, royally deliberate
In every gesture, the peacock
Is making his progress, pausing to peck
With a deeply sustained, slow, gracious indulgence
For his only audience:
Three crows on branches and me, respectfully quiet.

The sheen of his purple neck and turquoise breast, the amber
Disruptive coloration
Of his wings, his small unlikely crown
And even more unlikely train of a tail
(Whose eyes are catching all
The attention the crows and the sun and I can offer)

Make him seem rarified, more imperially barbaric
Than the apes and ivory
In the Primate and Elephant Houses here
At the zoo. He sees me sitting. Instead of veering
Away, as wise as a crow
Or as circumspect as a Solomon refusing

To risk his royal person on such an unpromising
Adventure, on one belonging
To my dangerous, endangered species,
He is coming straight my way, as if to demand
An immediate accounting
For some discrepancy in the treasure room.

With an effortless leap, he joins me at my table, no picnic
On it but himself, nearly

Within reach. I'm too awed to presume.
He stares with an onyx eyeball at the knick-knacks
From my poor tributary
Kingdom: a book, a camera, pieces of paper.

He waits a moment, expectant, indignantly condescending,
Then suddenly lets fly
His fearful, universally piercing
Announcement, his scream, his anguish at the end
Of Juno's and our world,
His simultaneously ecstatic and disgusted

Instant of pride and rancor and pain and non-amusement.
He preens while the crows answer,
Ridding himself of out-of-the-question
Pinfeathers in his train, remembers far loftier
Appointments, springs to earth,
And struts away on elegant spurred claws.

ᘄᘂ

*Cadenza*

Around you, the great composed resounding orchestra
Has fallen silent.
You wait. Everyone waits. The electrified conductor,
Hair still on end,
Nods and bows your way, holding his bent baton
Behind him, noting the gap
In the score where you alone must improvise a cadenza.
Fiddle on one knee
And bow on the other, the concertmaster listens, and all
The way through the choirs
To the dim assistant percussionist, as mute as his woodblock,
And all the way over
The heads of squirmers and program-rollers and gaping long-drawn
Yawners the silence widens
For this, your solo passage that should gather together
All that has gone before
And all that is yet to come in a florid rhapsodical flourish
Which only your virtuoso's
Fingertips can bring to the light of an inevitable
Unpredictable finale.
Everyone stares at you. The silence deepens. It lengthens.
Presto. The silence is yours.

# Three

## Return to the Swamp

To begin again, I come back to the swamp,
To its rich decay, its calm disorder,
To alders with their reddening catkins, to hummocks
Of marsh grass floating on their own living and dead
Abundance, and wait on the shore. From my shallow angle,
Even shallows turn solid: a cast-off sky,
A rough sketching of clouds, a bearable version
Of the sun in a mist, the upside-down redoubling
Of cattails, and my eyes, shiftless,
Depending on surface tension like water striders.

What did I hope to find? This crystal-gazing
Brings me no nearer what the mergansers know
Or the canvasbacks keeping their distance or the snipes
Whirring away from me, cackling, their beaks down-turned,
Heads cocked for my false alarm as they swivel
Loudly and jaggedly into the next bog.
Here among shotgun shells and trampled blackberries,
How can I shape, again, something from nothing?

Edgy and mute, I wait at the edge,
And a bass taking a fly — a splashing master,
Ringmaster of refracted light — remakes the world,
Rippling out beautiful exchanges of stress
And yield, upheaval and rearrangement, scattering
And then regathering the shards of the day,
And suddenly near, there, near in the water
Where he's been floating motionless all this hour,
The hump-browed bullfrog staring at me close-mouthed,
Fixing on me his green, princely attention.

## *Bittern*

Neck drawn in, dark shoulders
Hunched, the bittern alone
Among marsh reeds, its beak
A splinter pointed at clouds,
The stump of its brown body
Motionless, till now one gust
Of wind moves the dead stalks
Around it, the bittern swaying
Slowly like reeds, the long thin
Streaks of its breast moving
In time with wind, then slowing
To stillness, standing (barely
There) by water, waiting.

ᘖ

*Wading in a Marsh*

Nothing here in this rain-fed marsh
Has known the sun on the far side of the mountain
Except by the hearsay of the moon
Or the glinting of clouds and snow through cedar boughs,
And by this hand-me-down light I wade,
Uncertain of every surface preoccupied
By milfoil and watercress, the floating
Intricate uncannily green beds
Of water starwort whose leaves allow
No reflection of mine, not even their own.

My rake-handle staff goes first, searching
For footholds in the moss under the water,
In the soft debris of needles and spikerush
And mud and the good lost lives of burreeds,
And my feet follow, slow as the spawn of tree frogs.
The water-logged hemlock logs give way
Underfoot as easily as the earth they've turned to,
And my staff, at times, reaches down to nothing
As deep as I am tall. I don't go there.

Even with something seemingly lasting
Under me, I sink if I stand still,
Learning the underlying answer
Of swamps as unforgettably as my name:
To stand is to sink, to move is to rise
Again, and nothing at all has died in the winter
Without being reborn. The duckweed
Drifting against my thighs is rootless, unnerved,

Immortal, a cold companion
To be cupped in the palm and then let go
Here in Barr Mountain's permanent shadow.

I see what to say: this marsh that holds me
Is the climax of a lake, shallowing, dying,
Filled with the best endeavors of pondweeds,
The exploring and colonizing shapes of a world
Too good at living for its own good,
But in this man-made silence, while wrens and kinglets
Decide what I am and slowly excuse me
For being a moving object with much less use
Than a stump, I learn why I came here
Out of order: in order to find out how to belong
Somewhere, to change where all changing
Is a healing exchange of sense for sense.

I start to sink, I take a step,
The mud puts up with me momentarily,
And three wrens at once from three directions
Burst into songs as wildly interwoven
As white water crowfoot tripling itself in shade.
I have to stand still to listen. By the time
I've heard the spruce grouse drumming and drumming
Under the wrensongs, vibrant as memory,
I begin to sink. One winter wren
Appears from a literal nowhere: in her beak
A stark-green writhing caterpillar
Airborne ahead of its time. In an instant, she scans
The parts of me still above water,
Then vanishes among a tangle of roots
To feed her young. Far overhead
Sunlight crosses the treetops like crownfire,
And the last snow of a new spring
Melts as it falls, turning to other stars.

တေ

*Algae*

They are floating, suspended
In the still pondwater
Under the touching, the rippling
Of water striders, the hovering
Sheen of damselflies, not needing
To care where wind and sun
Are going, but drifting
Rootless and leafless, flowerless,
Their green translucent hair-thin
Bodies feeding and turning
On the long threads of daylight.

Now at the edging-over
Of winter, the first fall
Of whiteness, they settle
Downward, they soften, they gather
To rest, they darken
For a dark season, waiting
To lift new lives to their sky-pale
Likeness, to rise gently,
To mirror the spring rain.

## *Craneflies*

One skyward, one head-down
By the shaded pond, the craneflies
Are mating, their long ungainly
Silk-thin crooked legs are clinging
To the stems of quillwort, only
The frail ends of their bodies
Touching, motionless, their slender
Wings held motionless all day
Entranced, they have fallen
From their meeting in midair,
Their wind-tossed wind-lost
Encounter, now windless, they lie
As if dreaming of nothing
But the endless calm of evening.

## ᎨᎧ

*The Death of a Cranefly*

It falls from the air
Stricken, spiralling
Lamely, already dying,
Its arched inch-and-a-half
Of body trailing
The long disjointed-seeming
Legs out of sunlight
Onto the pond's dark water
Where swiftly a water strider
Clings to it, rippling
And skimming away with it over
Reflections of yellow leaves,
Holding one amber
Lace-ribbed lifeless wing
Aloft (a small sail
Disappearing among the quiet
Inlets of milfoil)
As buoyantly as a lover.

ง๛

## *Looking into a Pond*

The leaves have floated across the shallow pond
For days, yellow but darkening, and now
They fall a second time to the mud below

Where I see them lie like water churned by a storm,
The stems and the cupped blades nesting together,
Not moving, turning green again beneath algae

And mouldering under silt that will smooth them slowly
Away under the underface where air
And water touch, where still another surface

Comes down now at a slant to take my eyes:
The birdless, cloud-bearing, endless, cold, and coldly
Reflected sky where air and nothing meet.

മ്മ

*Caddisfly*


One by one it chose them
From the streambed, the sandgrains
And the smallest of smooth pebbles
To make the gray hovel
It wears, its inch of river
Joined fast together
And fitted close
By what flowed from its hearts,
A current within it, slow

As the current it breathes,
Clinging to stone and waiting
For its body to be long,
Longer, a slender stranger,
For their clear-netted wings
To be wings, and now they know
It is now, and now they let go
Of their thin shelter
And rise out of the water

Into a stream of air,
Dizzy and laggard, heavy
With what they are, and fly
In a hatching haze
Downwind and downstream
And fall as they fly to find
Whether they join still another
Or fall alone to the welcoming
Mouths under the river.

## *Dipper*

From water-swept stone
To stone it flies in a swift flutter, skimming
The surface, standing on stone again, dipping,
Dipping and staring from under its silver eyelids at the lunge
And spill of the stream it now slips under
Suddenly as if drowning, to disappear
Into white water, wing-swimming, wing-walking,

And shimmers gently out
Of the current, holding a twig-spun larva sheath,
Flutters to stone, dark stone-colored feathers
Stone-dry in rain and spray sweeping downstream,
Dipping and staring among red cedar roots, then flying
With rain and spray so near
Water, it needs no air underwing, now swerving
Under the waterfall to its nest, singing.

## Marsh Hawk

Along the split-rail fence, no higher
    Than a man standing, the hawk comes
Flying as jaggedly as the rails,
    Its wings touching them nearly the color
Of trees turned into weather
    By years, dead silent now, one wingbeat
For every swerve, eyes scanning
    The grass for gray deermice
Under the leaning posts, catching
    No shadow in that light as gray
As the sea wind, hearing nothing
    As sharply soft as its sudden cry, flying
Away, fence-riding crookedly, tilting
    From field to marsh to darkness.

ಌ

*Loon Feather*

It has plunged under the sea, this sea-gray feather.
It has gone flying
Under the sea more swiftly than fins, has swerved
And dived, risen to catch
Sunlight, gleamed like sunlight in full gales
When the waves rushed
Across its barbs their chaos and young night,
And has swept ashore
Over salt marshes, pinetrees, up mountain valleys,
Skimming sheer rock
To the edge of snow, to the spring ice-melt
Of this high lake
Where, against reed stalks, by feather-gray ripples,
It lies in its nest.

## ၇၂

*In Sand and Wind*


Between dunes, the dry, salt-whitened sand
Has blown away in the wind as deep as the water
Under it, and rooting there, a small coast willow
Is leaning upwind as if to follow.

Upright beside it in the rippling hollow,
A cottonwood has begun its second summer,
Dark stem aimed upward and dark roots deepening,
Leaving the willow slanting and giving in.

The dunes will come back to this brief garden, as surely
As the wind, and bury it. The willow will die
Easily, losing its leaves to a sun fading
Behind the sandgrains drifting along its branches.

The cottonwood, reaching deeper and stretching higher
To hold to water and the last of the light,
Will last for years, half-drowned, before going under
Like a mast in a calm sea, its last leaves waving.

ಬಬ

*Driftwood*

From its burial at sea, a gray-white forest
Has come to Dungeness Spit to lie ashore:
Whole trees, their bark long-lost, their roots clutching
Only the wind, their jumbled branches
Smooth-sided schools of fish.

Not one of the thousands, thousands strewn for miles
Across and among each other, gnarled or straight
Or broken, level, slanted or half-buried
In sand, not one though dead and left
For dead gestures of storms,

For masters of seawrack done with dying now
In the salted calm of knots and rings and veins,
In every cell still held out to the light
Or the rain, having no more to do
With stretching and letting fall,

Not one though leafless, the green gone, cast away
And stranded here like the bones of forgotten seasons,
The bones of the dying gods of moving water
And weather, under our eyes or fingers
Not one not beautiful.

ನುಡಿ

*Surf*

He woke to the strange sound of the sea, half dreaming
Of wind and storm, still landlocked, not knowing
Yet how to dream of surf without half waking
At its wash and rush, its slow going-away
To surge again as steadily as breathing
But wilder than that easy coming and going
And wilder than his uneasy heartbeats.

He lay in the dark, trying to soothe the ocean,
To rest it, to calm it, but it poured
Over and over him through the night, the waves
Like a storm pulsing and blowing among trees
And coming again to roar and breathe and beat,
Breaking against him, breaking against the shore
Of his mind swept white, foaming across his sleep.

## ⋈

*The Lost Stones*


They lie lost on the prairie, far apart
Among grass, not touching other stones
As on a riverbed or the side of a mountain.

The grass rises around them like green fire
Bending and wavering, the blades burning
And dying back, casting their small seeds.

And birds peck at the seeds. Pintails and quail,
Sparrows and buntings eat them, but some fall,
And from old roots, the dead begin again.

The lost stones wait while shoots and stalks and crowns
Rise up and flourish like ground mist in the morning,
Then scatter, settle, and fade into the night.

Under snow the stones will wait with fallen grass,
Feel the same rain but wait, feel the same sun
But wait and burn without seeming to burn,

Feel the same wind as the grass blowing against them
Without bending or toppling or turning darker.
No one will see the stones wearing away.

No one will see their seeds as fine as dust
Flying away in the wind or washing over
Their slowly smoothing edges into the earth.

## ᔕᔕ

*At the Edge of a Desert*

This is the end of ours and the beginning
Of a separate country, a quiet border
Distinct as a seashore: beyond, nothing as tall
As a man — pale ocotillo, catclaw acacia,
Cholla, and paloverde shrink
Deeper in thinning soil and sand
From the punishment of the sun, their branches
Give way in the distance, slenderer, give way
To smaller leaves, to hooks and spines, to the whiteness
Of salt, to sagebrush and the loneliness
Of creosote poisoning its own dry seedlings,
To shapes more solitary, leaning on nothing,
Depending on no others for shade, the shadscale,
Stem-swollen desert trumpet, finally
None at all on the breathless land, the levelling
Light gone flat in an Eden of bitterness.

ᘉ

## Staying Found

"We become lost not because of anything we do, but because of what we leave undone. . . . We stay found by knowing approximately where we are every moment. . . ."

— BRADFORD ANGIER, *How to Stay Alive in the Woods*

He stood alone on the almost washed-away road
By the rain forest, caught by its impossible
Greenness. He started walking toward it, bewildered
By a wilderness he'd only half imagined
Among the mills and ruined lakes of his childhood.

He walked on moss as deep as his strange shoes
More softly than he'd ever walked, more quietly
In a rain that fell without falling, through an air
Softer than water, on earth, on a resurrected
Earth whose fire was wildflowers, glistening
Suns and moons of berries, dawns of gold lichen,
And scarlet sporophytes like spearheads guarding
A nurse-log where young cedars rose from the graves
Of ancestors, once two hundred or more feet
Above his feet and theirs, where huge others
Had closed a sky between him and the sky.

He stood among small perfectly neglected
And cared-for children in a virgin forest
And found himself. But when he turned, he was lost.

One moment he had been healed. He had forgotten
The defeated trees, the flowers starving

72

In poisonous wind and rain, the dead ground
Where he had tried to grow. In another moment,
He had learned a different way of dying
Called Here and Now, called There and Where and Nowhere.

When he stumbled onto the road again, his mind
Had changed. He was no longer lost in the woods
Or in cities as he had always been,
Not knowing it. Now, he would stay found.

## The Other

He was alone in the woods. Then, in an instant,
He was not alone. He'd heard nothing different,
Seen nothing strange, felt no strange tremor
Under his feet, no touch on his shoulder.
But something else was there and was watching.

He stared at the trunks of firs, at vine maple
And devil's club, a thicket of salmonberry,
A deadfall covered with ferns and ice,
Orange cup fungus, liverwort, the rushing
Half-frozen creek beside him, and saw nothing.

Nothing to fear. Nothing he knew had changed
But his mind. He'd been standing in this place
To dream of it, to belong to it, hoping
To make a charm all winter against winter.
Suddenly he was empty. What he saw

Was empty. His mind had emptied. This part of the forest
Had lost him, had become only itself,
Turned stark and raw and bleak, and nothing living
Or moving in it belonged where it was or was going
To belong to anything else or anywhere.

The cold light of the sun seemed pitiless,
Cast down and away from him, the creek
Not the same water at any glance, and the trees
Dismembered, like him, the last of their kind.
The Other had moved into that emptiness.

He felt afraid. Saying the words out loud
Frightened him more, and panic, a snow shower,
Froze him where he was, while the Other stayed
Where it was and watched him trembling,
Unable to move, unable to wonder.

And then it was gone. Each stone, each drop of water,
Each leaf glittered alone. He was still
Standing where he had been, with what he'd thought
He half understood: a small piece of a world
That was his to keep. Now it was no one's.

ᏁᎯ

*Elegy for a Firtree*

Its life began naturally in the woods:
A fir seedling among thousands of others,
Only a few of which would be survivors.
The cone it came from
Fell to the duff, and one seed swelled and rooted,
Lifting a single needle-covered stem
Straight toward a zenith it knew even in darkness.

It lived under snow, branched in its second season,
And then the tree that had nurtured it came toppling
Down to the ground to the screeching of chainsaws,
Having been topped, then trimmed,
And finally bucked and hauled by chains, skidroaded
To a bleeding heap down-slope, leaving behind
The ruins of a forest scattered with orphans,

Most of which, crushed or stripped, died with their elders.
This one stayed half alive, though half the soil
Had abandoned its roots and its old heaven
Had turned to a horizon.
Yet it kept growing, curving its main stem
Toward a new calling: this mysterious
Godhead that could suddenly change the world

By a lurching quadrant in a terrible instant,
That could make each previous day of life seem wrong,
A mistaken choice, a misguided bearing
For the sense of direction
Firtrees bear in the hearts of their heartwood.

In its third year, it dealt with other gods
That had come to harrow hell: the bulldozers.

They passed so near it, gouging their logging road,
This still stunned hanger-on plunged upside down
But clung to its share of clay and shattered granite
Under the raw half-cave
Of a cutbank where it groped into half-light
And turned again to the sky, fighting its way
From under the hanging gardens of earth-movers.

I found that tree in its fifth overturned year
And dug it out of its grave, first-aided its body,
And planted it in a bowl like a *bonsai*
Or a *ne-agari*
With exposed roots, a rare quintupling of trunks
Which no harsh gardenmaster had to disfigure
Into a semblance of old age or wisdom.

It came by its gnarling honestly and grimly.
No thanks to anyone, it kept on living,
Stayed green for five tame years on a terrace,
Gathering moss, believing
In another zenith for a final time,
Nursing a spray of pearly everlasting.
Then it turned pale, clenching a small fist

Of roots, bewildered. Though I gave it freedom
With the whole earth under it in a flowerbed,
Its needles wilted and fell in a cold year.
Now it endures
One more odd twist away from the fate of firtrees:
Uprooted and wild and beautiful, even in death,
It stands in my workroom, pointing at the ceiling.

ᎣᎣ

*Black Bear*

Before I do it myself, already he's running
Away past stumps through bracken and huckleberry
And brambles, having seen my shape before
I froze at the sight of his, through slash
Bleached white as bones, downhill, blacker than shadows
Slanted along the ruts of the bulldozers
And under deadfalls, past slabbings and widowmakers
Whose jagged splinters snag at a gray sky,
Across raw earth near the edge of the clear-cut
And down into the last stand of this forest,
Still running, giving my body one calm glance
Over his shoulder, a look as supple and sure
As that shoulder, fearless, but wanting none of me.

ॐ

## Staying Alive in a Clear-cut Forest

I sit on a forest floor
That has lost its forest.
After five winters and Aprils
In the unaccustomed light
The groundlings have turned pale,
Wondering what and where
They are, having outlasted
One more dazzling summer:
Clubmoss and vine maple,
Bittercress, maidenhair,
Rush, sweet-after-death.

Around me, seedling firs,
Whose thick drought-toughened branches
Seem artfully dwarfed and maimed
By their masters like *bonsai*s
Or like wind-shaped, sidewise
Godchildren of crownfires,
Are groping toward the sky
Again among rotten splinters
And the gray slabs of their elders
Slowly, outgrowing my anger
In the sawteeth of disaster.

To learn from the survivors
Skills I can only pray for,
I come back year after year
Like one of the outlanders
Growing beside me — clover,
Stonecrop, vetch, star thistle —

The perennial common strangers
Who thrive when the shade goes,
Who cast a few small shadows,
Who struggle in fading light,
Who will die in a green darkness.

## Some Other Roads

"Two roads diverged in a wood . . ."
         — ROBERT FROST

He wanted a way where thinking would be the same
As walking, a road like many others, turning
Aside, not long, not far, not mindlessly level
But curving, slanting downhill, and he went there

By turning like many other walkers of roads
To a softer, darker, narrower lane where alders
Shaded the down-curved green of the hillside
And led him down to a streambank where he followed

Downstream a softening, narrowing pathway
Above the rush and plunge of water on stones
On a day that disappeared into each moment,
Streaming and spilling its own green-shaded course,

And stepping on watery stones, not rushing or plunging
Now, he turned aside at a deer-trail
And bowed under branches toward a slanted meadow,
Half disappearing like the daylight beside him,

And passed a gate as if he weren't thinking
Of anywhere long lost or far or passing
And, turning aside again, knelt down in grass,
As still as that meadow and the deer browsing.

81

## ∽

*Trying to Sing in the Rain*

I sit by a steep deer-trail rapidly becoming
A small rapids with runoff from the rain
Higher in the woods, trying
To make one kind of song. The water falling around me
Has its own ideas about singing. It keeps running
Into my mouth and ears
And babbling better than I can, halfway up this mountain.
The runnel is flowing under me through a culvert
Into a stony creek that plunges
To a waterfall at a concourse of two creeks, and that stream
Falls to the river I see through a stand of cedars,
That river meeting another
River and together stretching wide to the ocean,
And I stretch wide more narrowly than the least
Members of this deep-green
Watershed, the swordfern, lichen, and moss beside me,
Yet all of us here take in more than we know,
Their cells and my soaking page
Gone blurred, but my heart at every heartbeat full and empty
By turns, as full and empty as the sky
By turns of the day and earth,
So recklessly happy I don't care if I'm out of kilter,
Far offkey, or taking an offbeat beating
And pummelling from my teacher,
The openhanded god of the storm who gives me this wrung-out
Singing and floating lesson, sending what passes
For my roots more rain
Than I can imagine how to use and washing my words
Away like part of the tumbling bedload
Of some wild river-to-be.

## Four

ᬬ

*Total Eclipse*


Wearing awhile the corona of the sun
And not his pallid, changeable reflection,
The moon in the midst of day crowns herself queen.
We lift our eyes to the shadow of a stone.

## For a Woman Who Dreamed She Was a Mermaid

You woke in fear of scales and a fishtail,
Of waves cresting
Over a gray barnacle-crusted shoal
Where you were singing
Nothing, numb in the wind, not even combing
Your long soft hair with coral,
Forsaken by dolphins, the salt music of gulls
At the heart of your weeping.

Whatever you turn to now, by half or by whole,
Waking or sleeping,
I'll stay both lovers: the sailor half-seas-over
And over the railing
Floundering toward you, and the moon-eyed flounder waiting
And mooning for Neptune's daughter,
Both ready to take whatever joys you offer
In the air, underwater.

## Note with the Gift of a Bird's Nest

We watched them weaving it, pulling our long strands
Out of the hairnet hung on a bush, the bushtits
As small as wrens, mixing our mingled combings
With moss and spiderwebs they'd gathered while clinging
Upside down, chirping in wind and rain.
We should have been ashamed of ourselves at such
Barefaced sentiment, a Victorian notion
Fit for the Mauve Decade when human hair
Was braided and crocheted in doilies and bracelets,
Framed around Loved Ones, plumped into doll cushions,
Kept cool in the bosoms of pale ladies' lockets,
Or curled in the gold nests of gentlemen's watches.

But those two tiny gifted completely
Admirable birds, day after April day,
Kept threading my silver threads among your gold,
As embarrassing as the very idea
Might sound in years to come or decades to go.
They hatched eight young ones in this rainproof lovely
Hanging basket, surrounded by part of us,
Not worried at all, all summer, by our poor taste
Or literary lapses like this in which I can say
By the hair of our heads and the work of their beaks, I love you.

## For a Woman Who Doubted the Power of Love

Didn't I say the sun would cross the sky
Like a burning stone
And, like a burnt stone, fall in the evening
To light the pathway
Of the huge red stone of the moon rising
For our eyes only?
Didn't I say the moon would fade and leave us
Pale as our faces
Here at the end of night as we lie together
Under the drifting snow?
Didn't I say all snow would turn to water,
Each drop a flower,
That the sun would rise as molten as always
In time with birdsong
By the light of our moving arms in the morning?
My love, listen and learn
Once more how I did all this by the power
Of your heart and my heart.
How could the sky and these falling star-lit leaves
Catch fire without us?

ꠜꠚ

*Turning Back and Starting Over*

1

Our feet slow down by themselves, trudging reluctantly,
And we're stopping cold, even before deciding
To stop. And here we are:
For all these miles, we've been going the wrong way. That easy
Beautiful open down-sloped welcoming trail
Was a hanging valley,
And now we stand at the sheer, sheared-off edge of it, staring
Down on the green place where we wanted to be
But have no path to.
Like unfledged hawks on a nesting ledge, we test our eyes,
Keen for the promises of worlds beyond us.
There they lie
Out of our reach, the grasslands strewn with lakes, the sheltering
Orchards like windbreaks where we might have rested
For the rest of our days
Instead of travelling, no matter how lightly. So we turn
Around regretfully and begin retracing
Our steps, those carefree
Rambling paces we took for granted, each now a dead loss,
A taking-back of what we once believed in
Wholly, wholeheartedly.
We search for the faint record of slips of heel and toe
On this hard stretch, on these unimpressed stones,
Seeing little or nothing
Of what we thought was progress: a few bent weeds, grass leaning
The wrong way here and there in our memory
Though not in our honor,

Scuff-marks and all our slipshod blunders longer-lasting
Than any surefooted strides. What did we bring
To light or life? We put down
Only our feet, dislodged a few fragments, left some seedlings
Tilted out of their zenith-seeking longing
Temporarily.
Though we gave ourselves a name when we began — Explorers —
Now, starting over, we have two more to carry:
Backtrackers, Beginners.


2


We've returned to the place were we went wrong, seeing no sign
To mark the spot, no X to commemorate
Our long mistake,
And taking the first new step is as hard as the first step
We took as children, our hands held up in the air,
Believers praising
Our imminent rescue from all fours. Starting once more,
We have to forget how wrong we were back there
Or we might never
Move at all, but simply stoop or crumple, settling
For less and less in a heap, giving up, giving in
To the luxuries of failure,
Of never having to choose or try. Instead, we labor
Uphill, both forcing and reenforcing our share
Of haphazard fortune, wonders
Of a kind, here among greater wonders: all these boulders,
These astonishing stumbling-blocks where we don't happen
To stumble this time, believing
In beginner's luck all over again. We've forgotten
On purpose, successfully, how to fail
And don't remember
Anything but the pleasures of travelling on and on
Though they may lead us now into nothing more
Amazing than dead-endings.

ನ್ನು

*The Resting Place*

We'll find it at the edge of a forest
Where moss and ferns, no longer overshadowed
By trees, will yield to grass, where a small stream
Will make its way among hills, where hills sliding
Like cross-waves into valleys (more pale
As they give in to distance) will turn to mist
Under the jutting folds of mountains
Whitened against the sky or steepened to blue
As far as blue-white clouds. And we'll rest there.

At our feet, the water will move in a grave dance,
Dissolving its stones downstream and honoring
Each one in its way for paying an easy tribute.
Nearby, a thrust of rock will remind us
Of the hard start of the earth. The weeds and wildflowers,
The bushes and brambles rooted for lost seasons
Will lose their names in the flourishes of the wind,
And our two natures, lost in thought,
Will give themselves away and become nameless.

We'll find an end to sitting and thinking,
Even to holding still, though stillness will be
That end in itself. Our reclining bodies,
Our longing and belonging shapes, will need
Nothing, will have nothing to wait for,
But will share the sun with other surfaces
Out of their depth, our eyes and fingers
Catching the sky as it falls and scatters
Around us, against us, its extravagant light.

ನ

*Chorus*

That rain-strewn night in the woods, the *chorus, chorus*
Of the green tree frogs called us
And led us by flashlight far from our firelight
Over and down a logging road to the marsh,

And they kept singing as green as the half-frozen
Hemlock branches we brushed slowly among,
As high and thin as the air we tried to hold
As breath among mountains, as thin

And clear as the ice our boots were breaking
Gently, each step a pale-green croaking
Of its own, as we came nearer and nearer where
They had risen out of cold graves to the cold

At the brittle edge of winter broken toward spring
To make their music over a cold spawning,
To choir all night after night, telling each other
*We lived at the end of summer, we live*

*Here again and again.* As we came closer,
The singing ended, suddenly went silent
At a single pulsing throatbeat. Nothing but wind
And sleet made any sound over the marsh.

We turned our light away. We waited longer
And longer in darkness, shivering like the reeds
Beyond us, chilled as the film of ice at our feet,
Forgetting all words, and the first voice began

Again, far off, and slowly the green others
Nearby began their hesitant answers, their answers
Louder and clearer chorused around us
As if we belonged there, as if we belonged to them.

## ଇଛ

### By a Lost Riverside

The bedding stones, where we lay
All summer at low water,
Where we made our fires
And our love through fall and winter
And dreamed while gray-green
Rainbow-making salmon
Spawned as close as our arms,
Are gone now, carried downstream
By the changed course of the river.

Those earth-shapes on which we learned
To keep our balance (walking
Or lying down) have tumbled
Deep and have vanished
Side against smoothing side
Where only water-breathers
As cold as the current go
To find the riverbed.
We sit on the sheer bank.

The stream the Indians called
Sky reflects the sky
Of a darkening evening.
Love, remember: dry,
Those stones were gray, but in rain
Lay speckled like the eggs
Of wild, bountiful, barely
Imaginable birds
In an enduring nest.

ಬಬ

*Sleeping on Stones*


The stones of that riverbed wouldn't give in
Easily, wouldn't accept our bodies
Without a struggle, without being plucked out
By hand one at a time and moved
Over, out of the awkward way of our shoulders
And sides, our nonconforming members.

They were rounded smooth and, separately, seemed easy
To go along with, comfortable, as comforting
To the touch as polished carvings,
But the river had lodged them close and left them
Like the foundation of a ruin that nothing
But us at that moment would try to build on.

Beside us, in the shallows, a dog salmon
Was hard at her labor, flailing her tailfin
To shreds to make a hollow for spawning. Later,
She would drift downstream and ashore and lie
Still in a way that was still beyond us.
We cleared our way, restlessly watching her.

At last, we'd made our bed, and we lay in it,
Our eyes wide open like hers, but blinking then
(As hers never had, never would) and losing
Touch two eyes at a time, no longer moving
Stones but feeling as heavy as they were
And joining them in their dream, cold as the sun.

Those stones had found their places with all the help
The river could give them. We tried doing the same

Without the benefit of the current, only
The constant sound of its *Now* and *Now* and the salmon's
Way to follow. The water under our minds
Began to rise, began to come together.

It flowed over the gray stones in our skulls
That had been waiting, it rushed blue
And green and white, it smoothed them, it turned them
Speckled like constellations, it turned them over
And bedded them down, kept edging them stone-fast,
Shifted them, one by one, into one streambed.

And into that stream the salmon came, she swam,
Half turned, surged again, came closer,
Swivelled, and held against the flow, the color
Of sun on melting snowfields high among stones
Still in their mountain, she drank that snow,
She turned her shimmering side and began nesting.

ಬಌ

*Downstream*

We give in to the persuasions of the river, floating
Swiftly downstream as well as the leaves beside us,
Ahead of us, with little choice
Which way it may be next
That we find ourselves
One boat-length farther along, taking the rough with the smooth,
To the slackness of pools, down long, eddying riffles,
To the rush of spillways narrowing
And steepening suddenly
To white water
Where the river is leaving everything to chance and turning
Over and interrupting its own half-motions
Constantly in bursts and arches,
Mantling, spun into tendrils,
Its wild gestures
As memorable at a glance as marble but dying, reborn
Only another glance away, as the center
Of our attention, shifting at random
Everywhere like the sunlight,
Is caught by the play
Of light on all these surfaces, churnings and interweavings,
Upheavals, blossomings, an impulsive garden
Where we search and search as if for answers
And see its one reply:
Nothing is the same
Ever. This intricate bewilderment of currents,
In its least ripple, is unrepeatable.
The windbreak of alders we pass now,
The gravely leaning pale-boned
Row gone ashen,

Love, is another river, its bed channelled by seasons.
Our faces come near each other, mysterious
As water always. We cross a pool,
Translucent, the stones below us
Glimmering, remaining.

# Five

## A Sea Change

ᏃᏃ

*Going to Sea*

Since we're setting out to sea, everything in our world
Has suddenly one of two clear, separate names:
What We Leave Behind
And What We Take With Us. We have no need to rehearse disasters,
Like being wrecked and stranded, to choose our cargo.
We were born marooned,
Have been castaways all our lives, practicing the survival
Of our fittest, and now we know what's necessary:
Relics of our bodies
And souls, what's left of our minds, remnants of our hearts,
And something more weatherproof than our bare skins
To hold between us
And the sun, the rain, and the wind which keep no promises
And no appointments, but which will surely arrive
With or without our approval —
Add food and water, and we can subsist on these alone
After a dying fashion. We make our X
At the crux of departure
And bury there all we no longer treasure: death's-heads
Over bones crossing like sabres, a dead-man's chest,
Songs hollow as laughter,
Our pieces-of-eight and gold doubloons, our empty bottle
Left in the sand behind us, holding the message
Of our light parting breath.

ಬಿ

*At Sea*

We had always wanted to behave like the wind, moving
At its insistence slowly or quickly,
Obeying its impulse
Without regret under sails as full as clouds and taking
Gladly to heart its general direction.
The land disappears.
It sinks like an enormous ship. Even its mountains
Go back where they began, like us: under water.
Now our horizon
Levels the world, the mountains are made plain, and nothing
Is standing roughly upright except our mast
Which was once a tree
Among trees, its roots in a different element, growing
In the dark, opposed to changeable surfaces.
It answered gravely and lightly
The long calls of the earth and the zenith, and still aspires
But not to deeper or higher things: it leans,
It circles, quivers
As if ready to fall to the ax, shakily pointing
At the unreachable, unteachable sky,
Now there, now anywhere,
Trying to tell us too much but speaking only in whispers
Like its lost branches. If we knew where we were going,
It might be impossible
To get there with all this uncontrollable help from midair
And a tree whose needles have long since gone to ground
To find true north,
But having no destination makes our travelling easy
Going so far, so far. We should have forgotten
Long ago where to go.

ဘ

*Taking Our Bearings*


To find out where we are, we gaze at the sunset,
Then the moon and stars.
We bring their images down to touch the sea,
And there we are: there,
At a certain time where straight lines intersect
On a chart — that's you and I
In all this emptiness, the only two
In the world existing
Our way in this place. We can put our fingers
Surely on our uniqueness,
Call where-we-are what-we-are, letting it go
Finally that simply,
Saying again it's only the beginning
Again, it's only
The beginning of everything we always wanted
To do and know and be.
Bracing uncertain sea-legs, we breathe the salt
Of our own blood,
Pitching, heeling, and yawing with the unbreakable
Rules of this road,
And steer by constellations we needn't measure,
Name, or number.
One must keep watch now while the other sleeps,
Each dreaming of sharing
Dreams like our food or, through a dreamless night,
Sleeplessly waiting
For daybreak, sharing the naked love of dreaming.
It will mean we're becoming
Each other, replacing our dying mothers and fathers
And our own children,

Rocked in this wooden cradle of the deep,
By good dead reckoning
Leaving behind our streaming, luminous wake,
Sailing toward morning.

ಬಚ

*The Calm*

Drifting and mimicking the loss of the wind
With a loss of mind,
Left slack-sailed here in the sea, doing nothing at all
For days, we begin
Taking our lives uneasily. Only the daylight
And the cracked chronometer
Are moving. Though we turn away from the sun
Or rise under the moon
As if we were earth and tide, the rest is stillness.
If we broke our silence,
This palpable air would ripple obediently,
But our voices falter.
They melt on the sea, as brief as glints of starlight.
On the deep dry land
Why did we never think of the miles and miles
Under us, holding us?
Above half-leagues of water, we think of little
Else than how deeply
The two of us might sink, turning to food
For the thoughts of others.
We could have stayed on firmament, on a desert
Where water waves goodbye,
Goodbye, and vanishes, a plain where it flows
On its own slight journeys,
Or on mountains where we could watch it frozen, toppling
(Instead of us) down cliffsides.
But here we huddle, surrounded. From miles below,
Now, come the monsters
Toward the glassy calm around us, uncoiling,

Lifting kelp-ragged
Slime-scaled snag-toothed cold impossible heads,
Eyes filled to the brim
With blankness, breaching and hulking, slewing toward us
Where we drift like lures.
Though they come closer, closer, blurred in the dark,
They never strike, never
Loom, ravenous, never thrash the surface
To break this mirror.

ೲ

*Reading the Sky*

Look, love, the sky is full again, as full as our sails.
Not being weather-wise, we read the baffling
Language of that sky
Slowly and doubtfully. Some skillful mariner might know
The signs like the palms of our hands and tell us
What we must do today
To be ready for tomorrow, but we murmur the names
Of clouds as if they were friendly enemies
Not meant to be trusted
To go where they should go or not to disguise themselves
Suddenly in different masks and colors.
The sky reminds us
Of our unpredictable minds: irresolute, inconstant,
Oracular, full of a mysterious music,
Barren, well- and ill-tempered.
Though we can't make it reveal its future or our fortunes,
Here on the crests of waves that move us and move us
We can pay it honor:
We know its blues and reds, like our bodies, are born of dust,
Its whites and grays mere vaporings, its blackness
Concealed by dazzle,
But all this broken beauty of cloud-shapes, the endless
Promises and the unrepeatable gestures
Of light, omens, high masses,
Each shred, each smattering of each flamboyant sky-scape
Have numbed our language into a mawkish grandeur.
Though it may look absolute
For death to those beaten by storms, it can never be ugly
And never meager or miserly, always lavish
With unselfconscious praise

Of itself, even when empty. Let others people it
With hosts of maladroit gods, benign or vengeful,
Flinging stones or manna:
What it really is is gift and weapon enough. Though Heaven
Be lost or strayed or stolen, we have the heavens
Instead to venture beneath
From beginning to end, and though we come to the end of the earth,
The waterfall of the vanishing ocean, the dropping-off place,
We bear these heavens with us.

ᎧᎧ

## Landfall

Our boat aground, we bring slow feet ashore, and they sink
But not in sand alone. They keep believing
In the sea: they rise
And fall, not understanding. They won't agree with the land
Or each other, stumbling sideways in memory
Of the waves now breaking
Calmly and raggedly behind us. We're upright, and we seem
To stand, and we turn like worlds half free of the world,
Small moons spinning near
Our mother, earthbound but dazed by distance. Have we come home?
Is this where we were born? Is this where it was
All along, this place
Where, again, we must learn to walk? We wallow from the water
Like our hesitant helpless curious ancestors,
Taking our first taste
Of the different air and kneeling awash as if to pray
For trust in what holds us up less yieldingly
After a sea change,
No longer buoyant, bearing the burden of inescapable
Heaviness among strangers who are already
Shyly coming toward us,
Asking what seem to be questions in an unknown language.
Is it what we've always asked ourselves? *Who are you?*
*Can you be trusted?*
*What do you want?* They hold their hands behind them, hiding
Flowers or knives. Love, remember not caring
Whether this was the end of us
When we set out, embarking on new lives with nothing
To lose but our names? Now all turns nameless again

For us who must love to learn
Once more how to point at the trees and birds and animals
We see around us, even our own hearts,
Naming, renaming them.

ฆฆ

## Acknowledgments

*Antaeus:* In Sand and Wind
*Antioch Review:* Trying to Sing in the Rain
*The Atlantic:* Bears; Driftwood
*Bennington Review:* Squirrel; At the Edge of a Desert
*Chicago Review:* The Shooting Lesson; Staying Alive in a Clear-cut Forest
*Chowder Review:* Song from the Second Floor; Quiet
*Concerning Poetry:* Applying for a Loan with the Help of the *Dictionary of Occupational Titles;* Total Eclipse
*Country Journal:* Cutworm; Loon Feather
*Georgia Review:* Chorus
*Gramercy Review:* Cuckoo
*Harper's:* Marsh Hawk; The Resting Place
*Harvard Magazine:* My Path; Looking into a Pond
*Iowa Review:* Falling Asleep in a Garden
*Kayak:* In Distress
*Mid-American Review:* The Other
*Missouri Review:* Weeds; My Father's Garden; By a Lost Riverside
*Montana Review:* Whisper Song; Time Off for Good Behavior
*MSS:* Games
*New England Review:* Turning Back and Starting Over
*The New Yorker:* Nuthatch; The Garden of Earthly Delights; Return to the Swamp; Bittern; The Death of a Cranefly
*Northwest Review:* Dipper
*Oregon English:* Elegy for a Firtree
*Passwords:* Caddisfly
*Ploughshares:* In the Country of Old Men
*Poetry:* Under the Sign of Moth; Caterpillar Song; Spider Song; Moth Song; My Father's Ghost; My Physics Teacher; The Last Laugh; Palindrome: Inside Out; Wading in a Marsh; Note with the Gift of a Bird's Nest
*Poetry Now:* For a Woman Who Dreamed She Was a Mermaid; For a Jumping Spider; Craneflies
*Practices of the Wind:* Surf

*Prairie Schooner:* A Sea Change (all six parts)
*Quest:* For a Root-bound Rosebush; The Young Clematis; For a Woman
   Who Doubted the Power of Love
*Salmagundi:* The Arsonist
*Seattle Review:* Elegy Written in a Suburban Churchyard
*Telescope:* Black Bear; Some Other Roads
*West Hills Review:* Wild Clematis
*Western Humanities Review:* My Fire; The Lost Stones; Staying Found